LIFE SCIENCE PROJECTS for kids

PROJECTS IN GENETICS

Mitchell Lane
PUBLISHERS

Claire O'Neal

P.O. Box 196
Hockessin, Delaware 19707
Visit us on the web: www.mitchelllane.com
Comments? email us: mitchelllane@mitchelllane.com

Mitchell Lane
PUBLISHERS

LIFE SCIENCE PROJECTS for kids

A Project Guide to:
Exploring Earth's Biomes • Fish and Amphibians •
Mammals • **Projects in Genetics** • Reptiles and Birds •
Sponges, Worms, and Mollusks

The author gratefully acknowledges
discussions with Dr. Michael O'Neal.

**Library of Congress
Cataloging-in-Publication Data**
O'Neal, Claire.
  Projects in genetics / Claire O'Neal.
    p. cm. — (Life science projects for kids)
  Includes bibliographical references and
index.
  ISBN 978-1-58415-877-6 (library bound)
  1. Genetics—Juvenile literature. 2. Biology
projects—Juvenile literature. I. Title.
  QH437.5.O54 2011
  576.5078—dc22
                                    2010030898

Printing 1 2 3 4 5 6 7 8 9

CONTENTS

GENETICS

Imagine a drug the size of a single molecule that can cure cancer. Imagine ordering an exact, living copy of your pet after it dies. Imagine catching a criminal on the FBI's Most Wanted List using a single drop of blood. Does this sound like science fiction? It's not. It's how genetics is changing our world.

Genetics is the study of how **genes** work within an organism. Genes are specific sections of DNA, short for **deoxyribonucleic acid**. DNA acts like a biological record book, containing all the information an organism needs to grow and function on a daily basis. A copy of your DNA is found in each and every one of the millions of cells in your body. When you grow up and have kids of your own, they will have genes from your DNA in their cells, too.

Though genetics easily explains why children look like their parents, these answers are surprisingly new. In the 1860s, Austrian monk Gregor Mendel studied how physical characteristics, or **traits**, were passed down from generation to generation in pea plants. Mendel reasoned that "factors" passed the traits from parent to offspring. Each pea plant, he said, had two copies of each factor—one from the mother plant and one from the father plant. Scientists of Mendel's time thought he was crazy. In that day, scientists believed only what they could observe in the world around them. Mendel's "factors" were too small to be seen, hidden within each living thing. It wasn't until 1900—sixteen years af-

Character	Dominant Trait	x	Recessive Trait
Flower color	Purple	x	White
Flower position	Axial	x	Terminal
Seed color	Yellow	x	Green
Seed shape	Round	x	Wrinkled
Pod shape	Inflated	x	Constricted
Pod color	Green	x	Yellow
Stem length	Tall	x	Dwarf

Gregor Mendel derived the rules of inheritance by studying how different traits in pea plants were passed from generation to generation.

ter Mendel's death—that three European scientists confirmed his work.

Today, our understanding of everything in biology depends on Mendel's ideas. We now know that Mendel's "factors" are genes. Genes control everything about your body. They dictate the color of your skin, hair, and eyes. They determine how fast you grow. They even control certain aspects of your personality and your likelihood of developing cancer. The existence of genes explains so much about us, about what it means to be human, that scientists are racing to learn more.

But genetics also raises serious concerns. Should scientists be able to **clone** humans? Should personal DNA information be kept private? Can some genes make humans better? How far will we go to learn about ourselves on the **molecular** level?

In this book, you'll find fascinating projects, demonstrations, and experiments you can do at home to find out more about genetics. Many use common materials you probably have around your house. Each project has a simple setup, but also encourages you to ask questions, providing ideas to take your understanding to the next level. Be sure to keep track of your experiments and observations in a science notebook. Whether for a school project or just for fun, you'll learn about genetics, biology, and science in general. Let's get started!

Gregor Mendel

OBSERVING INHERITANCE HYBRID GUMMI-BEARS

Gregor Mendel loved to garden. As he tended to his pea plants, he wondered why some grew yellow peas and some grew green. Mendel decided to experiment, using pollen from one type of pea plant to fertilize, or **cross**, another. When Mendel crossed a purebred yellow-seeded pea plant with a purebred green-seeded plant, he expected to see yellow-green peas in the daughter plants. People in Mendel's day believed parents' traits blended, like paints, to make offspring.

To Mendel's surprise, the resulting seeds were all yellow. When he bred that generation of **hybrid** plants with each other, the next generation recovered the green type, yielding both yellow-seeded plants and green-seeded plants. It was as though the information to make green seeds lay hidden through a generation. In this second generation, however, green-seeded plants occurred in only one out of every four plants.

Mendel discovered that the gene for seed color in peas was controlled by two **alleles**, or varieties of a single gene. A daughter plant received one allele from each parent. In order to be green-seeded—the

recessive trait—a plant must be **homozygous** for the green-seeded allele—it must have two copies. Yellow seeds were **dominant**; if the daughter was **heterozygous**, inheriting both a yellow and a green allele, the yellow allele masked the green one. Since each parent allele had a 50-50 chance of getting passed on, Mendel realized that the seed color of the offspring was governed by probability, much like flipping a coin.

In the following experiment, perform a hybrid cross between pure-bred Red-Skinned Domestic Gummi-Bear candies and albino, or colorless, Gummi-Bear candies.

Materials
- pencil
- paper
- red Gummi-Bear candies
- white Gummi-Bear candies
- 2 paper bags or coffee cans
- 2 coins

Instructions
1. The cross begins with purebred parent bears. Each is homozygous for an allele—Red-Skinned Gummi-Bear candies have two red, and albinos have two white. Count out an equal number of red and white Gummi-Bear candies, each representing one allele from a parent. Put red bears in one parent container and white bears in another.
2. Choose one Gummi-Bear candy from each container. Record which alleles you picked in your notebook: R for red, W for white. Repeat this step a few times to create a generation of offspring. Only if you pick 2 Ws can the offspring be white. What color is each offspring?
3. Empty both parent containers of purebred alleles, and create the next generation by crossing two hybrid (RW) Gummi-Bear candies. Add equal numbers of both red and white Gummi-Bear candies to each container. Repeat step 2 and record your results. How many homozygous red, homozygous white, and heterozygous red resulted? What percentage of this generation will be red? White?

Parents

RR   X   WW   R   R

DRAW   R   W

1   6

2   7   W   W

3   8

4   9

Crossing purebred Gummi-Bear candies (RR x WW) produces only hybrids (RW). Mendel's real genius lay in analyzing what resulted in crossing the hybrids (RW)—a predictable mixture of RR, WW, and RW.

TROY GRANITE Granite Countertop

Coin flips

H= heads

T= tails

1 HT

2 TT

3 HH

4 HT

5

Much like the 50/50 outcome of a coin toss, dominant and recessive traits are inherited according to probability.

5. To put a hybrid cross in the simplest of terms, flip two coins at a time. Record your results. How often do you get homozygous heads? Homozygous tails? Heterozygous heads and tails? Compare these results to your Gummi-Bear candies breeding experiment.

HERITABLE TRAITS IN HUMANS DOMINANT VS. RECESSIVE TRAITS

In humans, a few interesting and easily observed traits follow a dominant/recessive pattern.

Trait	Dominant Phenotype	Recessive Phenotype
Widow's peak	Peak	No peak
Cheek dimples	Dimples	No dimples
Face freckles	Freckles	No freckles
Tongue rolling	Yes	No
Earlobes	Free	Attached
Cleft chin	Cleft	No cleft
Finger hair between first and second knuckle	Hair	No hair
Hitchhiker's thumb	Straight	Curved
Crossed hands	Left thumb on top	Right thumb on top
Hallux (toes) length	Second toe longer than big toe	Big toe longer than or equal to second toe

If a person has a dominant allele, the dominant trait, or **phenotype**, shows itself. With two recessive alleles, the person displays the recessive phenotype. The boy with freckles, Leonardo DiCaprio's widow's peak, the girl who can roll her tongue, the free-hanging earlobe—all display the dominant phenotype for their trait. See for yourself how these traits occur in the people around you.

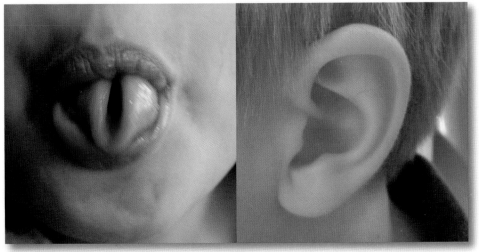

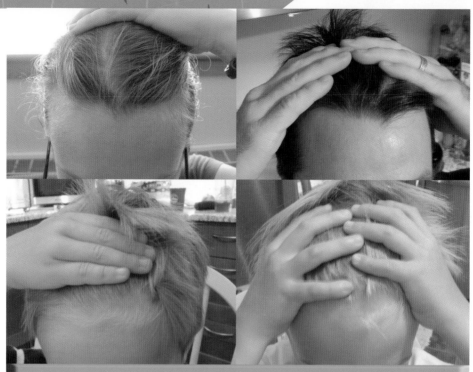

Hairlines of parents and their two sons. The father and older son (both right) have a widow's peak; the mother and younger son (both left) do not.

Materials
- paper
- pencil
- at least 20 interview subjects (classmates, family, neighbors)
- graph paper

Instructions
1. Make a chart to record the names and phenotypes of your interview subjects. Determine your phenotype for each trait, and record it in the chart.
2. Interview others to find out their phenotypes for each trait.
3. Using graph paper, make a separate bar chart for each trait to see how frequently the phenotype occurs.
4. Given a very large population, simple Mendelian traits occur at a ratio of 3 dominant phenotypes for every 1 recessive phenotype. Do your results show this pattern, too? If not, can you think of why?

INHERITANCE

Individual genes work together to create the phenotypes we see. The genes that make a phenotype for a particular trait are called its **genotype**. Use the phenotypes you observed in the previous experiment to determine your friends' genotypes for dominant/recessive human traits. On paper, pair your friends off and use probability to determine what their babies will look like!

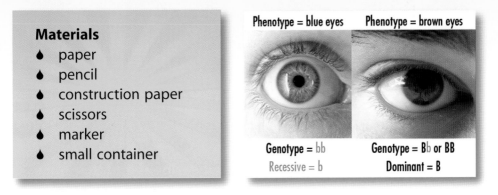

Materials
- paper
- pencil
- construction paper
- scissors
- marker
- small container

Phenotype = blue eyes   Phenotype = brown eyes

Genotype = bb   Genotype = Bb or BB
Recessive = b   Dominant = B

Instructions

1. Choose a letter to represent each genotype. Take a cleft chin, for example. The genotype *CC* or *Cc* creates a cleft chin, while *cc* does not.

2. Use the information of two individuals from the previous experiment and determine their genotype. If they have the dominant phenotype, you may not be able to say for sure, since their alleles could be homozygous or heterozygous. Write out which alleles could have created their phenotype for each trait.

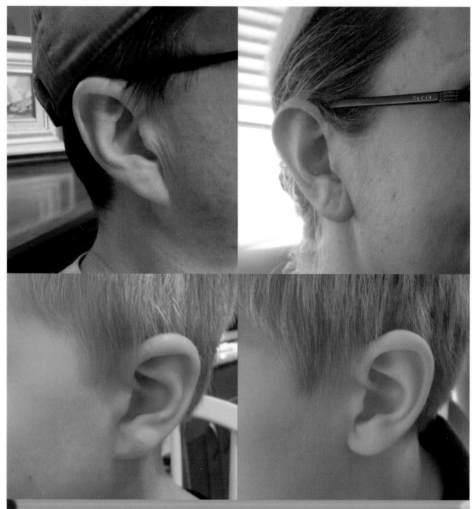

Earlobes of parents and their two sons. The father and older son (both left) have attached earlobes and therefore the recessive genotype ee. The mother and younger son (both right) have free earlobes, but must have the genotype Ee (the mother cannot be EE or both sons would have free earlobes; the son must carry an e gene from the father).

3. Pick a color of construction paper for each trait (example: orange for cleft chin), and cut out four small squares. These will be the **gametes** of your two individuals. Label each square with one allele from your two individuals. For example, if Person 1 has a cleft chin, write a *C* on one square. On the other square, write *C* on one side and *c* on the other. If Person 2 lacks a cleft chin, write *c* on two of the squares.

4. Time to cross-breed! Place the four gametes in the container, shake it around, and pick out two. Record your results. If you pick the square that has writing on both sides, go with the side you saw first. Each side has an equal chance.

Repeat for each trait to get the genotype for a possible offspring from these two people. What will the offspring's phenotype be? Feel free to draw a picture and fully embarrass your friends!

NATURE + NURTURE = VARIATION

While dominant/recessive traits are relatively easy to understand, most inherited traits are much more complicated. For example, you know that height is inherited; tall parents tend to have tall kids. But tall parents do not always have tall kids, and often siblings are not the same height.

Growth in humans is not always predictable. Genes, or "nature," play a role, certainly. Several different genes can all influence a trait's phenotype. But what goes on outside the body while it grows, called "nurture" is also important. Diet, health, and environmental conditions—such as smoking and pollution—all affect how people grow.

Given a certain genetic starting point, nature and nurture work together to determine the end result. If you could measure the height of everyone your age in the world, you would see enormous variation— tall kids, short kids, medium-sized kids. However, natural variation that can be measured always follows a certain pattern, called a bell curve. Learn more about the bell curve and variation among kids you know.

Materials
- at least 20 human subjects of similar age; more is better
- 7-foot tape measure
- pencil
- paper, preferably graph paper

Instructions
1. Measure and record the height, in inches, of each of your subjects.
2. Make a bar graph of the height of your subjects as a population. Label the x-axis HEIGHT IN INCHES and the y-axis NUMBER OF SUBJECTS. Plot your data on the graph. For example, if three of your friends are 45 inches tall, make a dot or color bars up to where 45 inches on the x-axis intersects with 3 on the y-axis.

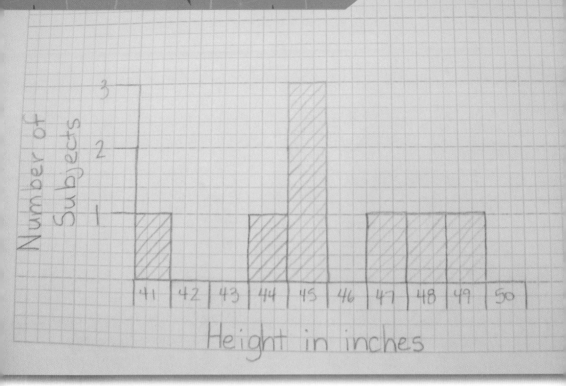

Number of Subjects

Height in inches

3. Carefully draw a smooth line connecting the dots or tops of the bars. If you have a large enough number of subjects, the line will form a bell-shaped curve—high in the middle, low on either end.

4. Calculate the average height of all your subjects. Find this height on your curve; it should be near the middle of the bell. How many inches shorter from the average height is the shortest subject? How many inches taller than average is the tallest subject? Notice how the shortest and tallest subjects are on the edges of the bell.

5. The bell curve simply tells us that most individuals are close to an average height, but that there are always outliers who are shorter or taller than average. If you don't see a bell curve, try to include more subjects until you do. How many people do you need to measure to see a bell curve?

6. Any measurable trait that has both nature and nuture components will display a bell-shaped distribution over a large population. Repeat your experiment with other physical traits, such as arm length or hand size. You could also measure physical abilities such as jumping distance or how long one can hold one's breath. Can you think of others?

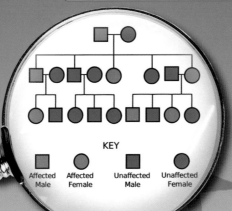

KEY

■	●	■	●
Affected Male	Affected Female	Unaffected Male	Unaffected Female

MAKE YOUR OWN PEDIGREE

Geneticists track how a trait is inherited over several generations using a special chart called a pedigree. You can make your own pedigree using what you already know about your family.

Instructions

1. Draw your pedigree as a kind of family tree on a sheet of paper. In pedigrees, females are represented by circles and males by squares. The oldest

Materials
- family members
- family pictures (optional)
- large sheet of paper
- pencil

generation (your grandparents or earlier) goes at the top; the youngest generation (you and your siblings) at the bottom. Connect married individuals with a horizontal line. Children are "produced" from that horizontal line by drawing a vertical line down to create a new generation on a lower level. Each group of siblings is shown in birth order from left to right. Here is an example pedigree of the author's family. Her grandparents are generation I; her children and her nephew are generation IV.

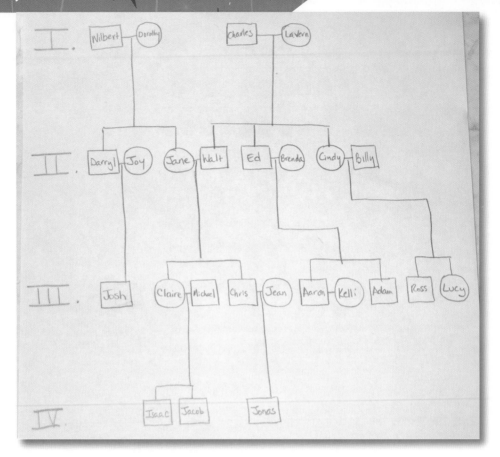

Make your pedigree go as far back and include as much detail as you wish. You may even want to attach family pictures. Leave space to record the traits you choose for step 2.

2. Pick one or two traits that run in your family—such as eye color, hair color, height, or baldness. You might also choose a medical condition, such as heart disease, nearsightedness, diabetes, or asthma.

3. Research how the traits you chose appear in your family by talking to your relatives and/or looking at family pictures. Don't be afraid to call older relatives. They are a treasure trove of information about older generations. Your pedigree will be most helpful if you can get information about every individual, but a few unknowns are okay.

4. Look closely at the traits you (or others) observed. Can you identify any patterns? Do you think some traits might be dominant while others are recessive?

5. If you couldn't determine a trait for a specific individual, can you predict what it might be now?

Friedrich Miescher

DNA UP CLOSE
EXTRACT A
DNA SAMPLE

DNA was discovered in 1869 by Swiss scientist Friedrich Miescher. He obtained his sample from pus on bandages he found in hospital trash! Before Miescher, most scientists believed that a cell's **nucleus**—the brain of the cell—contained mostly protein. While Miescher found protein, his ground-up cell nuclei contained enormous amounts of deoxyribonucleic acid, a strange, stringy white substance. Nobody knew what DNA's role was until 1952, when the American team of Martha Chase and Alfred Hershey proved that DNA was genetic material.

Separating DNA from Other Cell Material

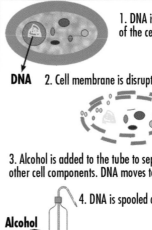

1. DNA is in the nucleus of the cell.

DNA 2. Cell membrane is disrupted with detergent.

3. Alcohol is added to the tube to separate DNA from other cell components. DNA moves to the alcohol layer.

4. DNA is spooled onto a glass pipette.

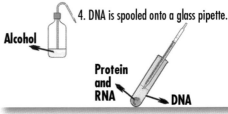

Alcohol

Protein and RNA

DNA

You can extract DNA just like Miescher, but using groceries instead of garbage. This experiment uses strawberries, but an equal amount of DNA-rich foods—dried split peas, bananas, kiwi, spinach, broccoli, chicken or fish eggs, or chicken livers—will also work. If you use chicken or eggs, be sure to wash your hands thoroughly with soap and hot water when you are done.

Materials
- 100 grams (4 ounces) of food sample, such as strawberries
- $\frac{1}{8}$ teaspoon (less than 1 milliliter) salt
- 1 cup (200 milliliters) cold water
- blender
- timer
- strainer
- measuring cup (pint-size or larger)
- 2 tablespoons liquid detergent
- test tubes or small glass containers
- meat tenderizer
- glass stirring rod
- ice-cold rubbing alcohol
- wooden stick
- small container that can be sealed

Instructions

1. Add strawberries, salt, and cold water to the blender. Blend on high for 15 seconds, until the mixture looks like runny soup. This will split open the strawberry DNA along with other molecules. Salt makes DNA clump together, though on a scale too small for you to see.

2. Pour the mixture through a strainer into a measuring cup. Discard the strainer's contents. Add 2 tablespoons of liquid detergent

to the measuring cup and stir gently. Let the mixture sit for 10 minutes to allow the detergent to break apart any remaining cells.

3. Transfer the mixture to test tubes, filling each $1/3$ of the way. Add a pinch of meat tenderizer to each test tube. Mix very gently with a glass stirring rod—stirring too hard at this step will break the fragile strands of DNA.

4. Tilt a test tube and slowly pour cold rubbing alcohol down the side. The alcohol will collect on top; add enough to equal the thickness of the water layer.

5. A thin layer of stringy-looking white fluff will form where the layers meet. This is DNA! Salty, clumped-up DNA precipitates out of solution in the presence of alcohol. Scoop it out of the tube with a wooden stick or a straw. You can preserve it in a small container of alcohol.

6. Try repeating this experiment with different DNA sources.

DO NOT eat this experiment!

BUILD YOUR OWN DNA MODEL

If you could look closely at the arrangement of atoms in DNA, what would you see? In 1953, nearly 100 years after its discovery, scientists Francis Crick and James Watson unveiled DNA's molecular structure. They discovered that DNA is a long, two-stranded, twisting ladder. The sides of the ladder, called the backbone, are made of phosphate and a special sugar called deoxyribose. Extremely stable chemicals called **bases** make up the rungs. DNA bases are adenine (A), guanine (G), cytosine (C), and thymine (T). Interactions between the base

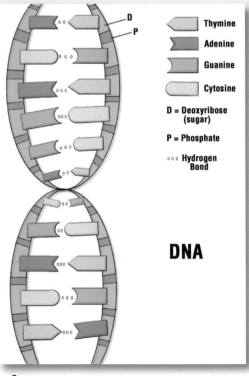

D
P

Thymine

Adenine

Guanine

Cytosine

D = Deoxyribose
(sugar)

P = Phosphate

∘∘∘ Hydrogen
Bond

DNA

James Watson (left) and Francis Crick explain their model of DNA, for which they won the Nobel Prize in 1962.

pairs hold the two DNA strands together, like teeth in a zipper. A always pairs with T; G always pairs with C. Taken in order, the sequence of bases reads like an instruction manual to the cell, providing all the operating instructions an organism ever needs.

Re-create Watson and Crick's exciting discovery by making your own delicious 3D model of DNA.

Materials
- rope-style licorice (such as Twizzlers)
- mini marshmallows
- 40 Gummi-Bear candies, 10 each of four different colors (such as red, green, orange, and yellow)
- toothpicks

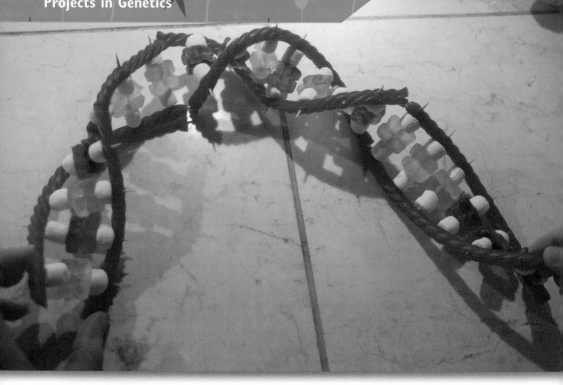

Instructions

1. Create 20 base-pairs using Gummi-Bear "bases." Make up your own base-pairing rules (such as red with green, orange with yellow). Push each pair into the middle of one toothpick so that the bears are touching.

2. Bond the "bases" to "deoxyribose" marshmallows. Push one marshmallow onto each free toothpick end.

3. Build the "phosphate backbone" out of licorice rope. Lay out the 20 toothpicks parallel to each other. Attach one licorice rope to each side of the toothpicks. If necessary, attach more licorice using toothpicks. Repeat, adding a backbone to the other side of the bases.

4. DNA makes a complete turn about once every 10 base-pairs. Carefully twist your model to see how DNA spirals.

Now that you know the basics, you can make a longer-lasting DNA model out of different materials. Chenille stems, drinking straws, or yarn can stand in for licorice. Wire or straightened paper clips make good bonds. Cardboard, packing peanuts, beads, or Tinkertoy building pieces would make good deoxyriboses or bases. Use your imagination to make an eye-catching model!

Telophase

MITOSIS

Each cell in your body has an identical copy of your **genome**, a complete set of DNA. The human genome contains over 3 billion DNA base-pairs. Each human genome has to fit into a nucleus, a cell compartment 5 millionths of a meter in diameter. To do this, the DNA is wound and packaged tightly into 46 **chromosomes**—two copies of 23 separate DNA units. One copy of each chromosome comes from the mother; the other from the father.

Your body makes new cells every day to grow, or to replace dead or worn-out cells. An old cell uses **mitosis** to divide and produce two new daughter cells. To ensure that each daughter cell ends up with a complete set of DNA, mitosis follows a series of steps:

1) Exact copies of all chromosomes are made.
2) **Prophase**: Each long, stringy chromosome condenses, packing tightly upon itself. A chromosome and its copy become loosely joined by a **centromere**. The wall of the nucleus that cages the DNA breaks apart.
3) **Metaphase**: All chromosomes line up in the center of the cell.
4) **Anaphase**: The two chromosome copies—called **sister chromatids**—separate and travel to opposite sides of the cell.

5) **Telophase**: The cell divides. New nuclear walls form around each set of chromosomes.

To learn about mitosis in a hands-on way, make a model of the stages of mitosis from a sock monkey. Sock monkeys have a "sockosome"—a genome made out of socks. If you can, take pictures at each step.

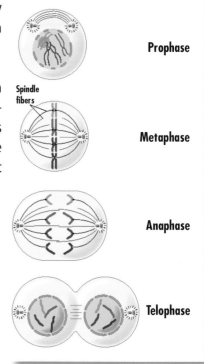

Prophase

Spindle fibers

Metaphase

Anaphase

Telophase

Materials
- 2 pairs of white socks
- 2 pairs of black socks
- masking tape
- yarn
- scissors
- camera (optional)

Instructions
1. Mark one pair of each color using tape. The taped pair of socks was inherited from the sock monkey's father; the untaped from its mother.
2. Form a large cell wall using a strand of yarn. Within the cell,

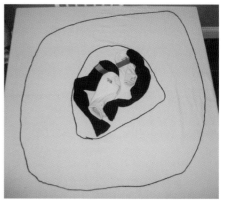

Cell growth (G phase)

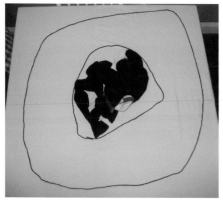

DNA replication (S phase)

use a smaller length of yarn to make the nuclear wall. Lay one member of each sock pair inside the nuclear wall. This represents the cell in growth phase, where it spends much of its life.

3. Replicate your sockosomes by stuffing the second sock of each pair into the nucleus. It's getting crowded; must be time for mitosis.

4. **Prophase**: Form a centromere to keep your matching sockosomes together by taping each pair together at the heels. Snip holes in the nuclear yarn wall.

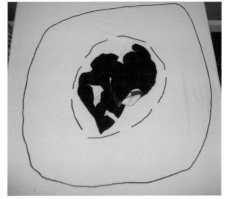

Prophase

5. **Metaphase**: Clear away the nuclear yarn. Line the sockosome pairs at the middle of the cell, as though a straight, vertical, imaginary line were running through each pair at its centromere.

6. **Anaphase**: Snip through the centromere. Separate the matching sockosomes from each other, pulling them to opposite ends of the cell wall. Begin pulling the top and bottom of the cell wall toward the middle.

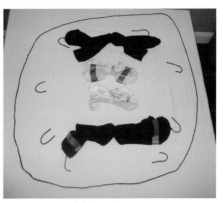

Metaphase

7. **Telophase**: Pinch off the cell wall, cutting it and retying it to make two new cell walls. Make new nuclear yarn walls in each cell around the sockosomes.

8. If you took pictures of each stage, print them out and assemble them into a flip book or use them to make flash cards.

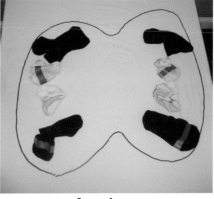

Anaphase

9. Use your model to analyze what might happen to the daughter cells if something went wrong at each stage of mitosis. What if mitosis began before the DNA was copied? What if one or more chromosome pairs did not separate during anaphase?

Telophase II

MEIOSIS

Mitosis creates two daughter cells that have the same number of chromosomes as the parent cell. All cells in your body replicate using mitosis, except for male and female sex cells. Sex cells undergo **meiosis** instead, because they must have 23 chromosomes, half the DNA needed to make a body cell. When sperm meets egg, they combine to give the new zygote 46 chromosomes, the exact amount of DNA present in the body cells of each parent.

Learn more about the steps by revisiting the sockosome activity.

Materials
- 2 pairs of black socks
- 2 pairs of white socks
- yarn
- scissors
- masking tape

Instructions

1. Repeat steps 1-3 of the sockosome activity, taping off the father sock, creating a cell, and replicating its DNA.

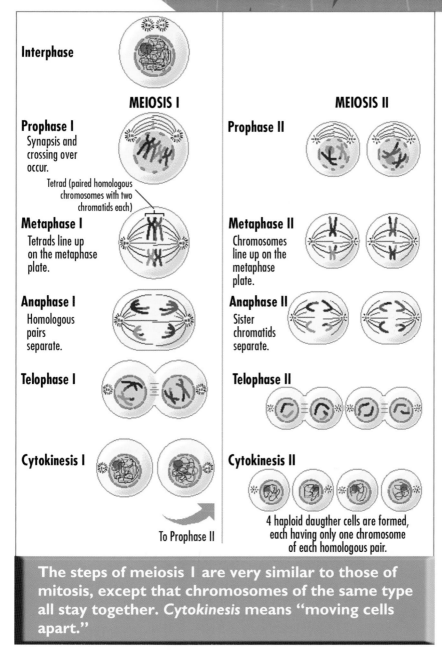

Interphase

MEIOSIS I

Prophase I
Synapsis and crossing over occur.

Tetrad (paired homologous chromosomes with two chromatids each)

Metaphase I
Tetrads line up on the metaphase plate.

Anaphase I
Homologous pairs separate.

Telophase I

Cytokinesis I

To Prophase II

MEIOSIS II

Prophase II

Metaphase II
Chromosomes line up on the metaphase plate.

Anaphase II
Sister chromatids separate.

Telophase II

Cytokinesis II

4 haploid daugther cells are formed, each having only one chromosome of each homologous pair.

The steps of meiosis I are very similar to those of mitosis, except that chromosomes of the same type all stay together. *Cytokinesis* means "moving cells apart."

2. **Prophase I**: Create a centromere for each pair of sockosomes by taping them at the heel. Intertwine each sockosome pair with its duplicate—black sockosomes snuggle up with black, white sockosomes with white. Snip the nuclear yarn wall to pieces.

3. **Metaphase I**: Slide the quartets of sockosomes to the cell center, aligning their centromeres vertically as before.

4. **Anaphase I**: Separate the sockosome quartets, moving the mother pair to the opposite side of the cell from the father pair. Begin to pinch the cell wall in the center.

5. **Telophase I**: Pinch, snip, and retie the cell wall to create two new daughter cells. **Notice**: Unlike mitosis, each daughter cell has half the genetic information as the parent cell, because the father's chromosomes split from the mother's. In some species of sock monkey, the nuclear yarn wall re-forms in the daughter cells and some time passes before stage II of meiosis. Other species cut right to the chase.

6. **Prophase II**: The matching socks are still joined at the heel. If the nuclear membrane re-formed, snip it to pieces.

7. **Metaphase II**: Line the sockosome pairs up in the middle of the cell, as in mitotic metaphase.

8. **Anaphase II**: Snip the centromeres and pull each sockosome from

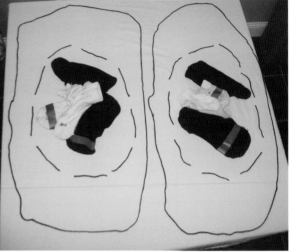

Prophase II

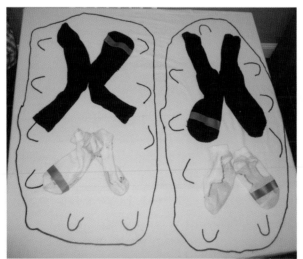

Metaphase II

its partner, toward opposite ends of the cells. Begin to pinch each daughter cell wall at the center.

9. **Telophase II**: Pinch the middle of each cell wall together, snipping and retying to form two new daughter cells from each cell from step 1. Now you will have four daughter cells, each with

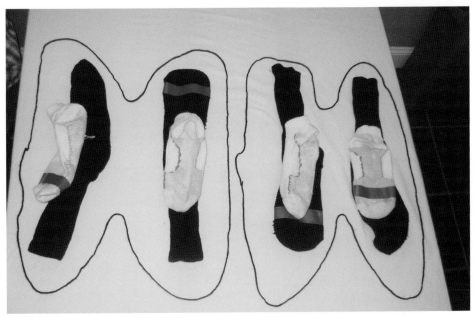

Anaphase II

half the genetic material of its parent. Re-form the nuclear yarn membrane in each cell around the sockosomes.

10. What could go wrong at each step of meiosis, and what would happen to a zygote if those errors occurred? Down syndrome is a genetic condition that occurs when a zygote contains three copies of chromosome 21 instead of the normal two. Which stages in meiosis could create sex cells that may result in Down syndrome?

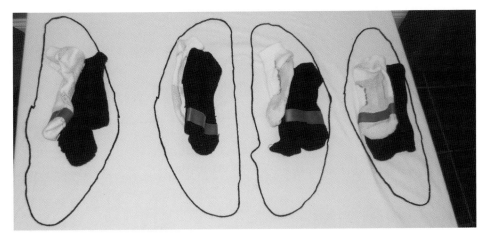

Meiosis II: 4 daughter cells

DNA REPLICATION

Before mitosis or meiosis, cells copy their DNA. A group of proteins called **DNA polymerase** performs this task. First, DNA polymerase unzips the double helix. One at a time, the protein machine "reads" the bases on the old DNA and matches new bases to each side. Finally, DNA polymerase bonds the phosphate backbone of the new base to the growing strand. DNA polymerase is both fast and accurate, making an average of only one mistake in every billion base pairs.

When mistakes do happen—inserting the wrong base, skipping one, or inserting too many—these **mutations** change the sequence of DNA. Some mutations are harmless; some are fatal. Cancer, for example,

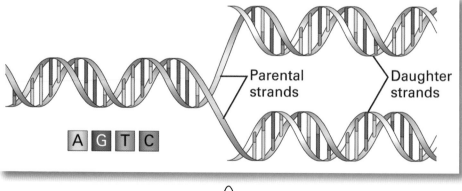

Parental
strands

Daughter
strands

A G T C

occurs when mutations cause the regions of DNA that control mitosis to malfunction. Many inheritable genetic diseases result from simple mutations. Changing a single base from A to T in the middle of the gene for the blood protein hemoglobin, for example, causes sickle cell anemia.

DNA polymerase has a daunting task. Give this hardworking machine a break and take over.

Materials
- pencil
- construction paper
- scissors
- marker
- yarn
- tape

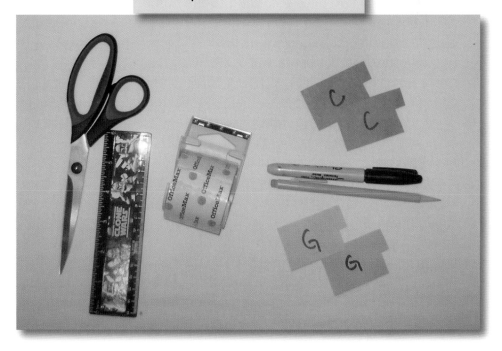

Instructions
1. Write out a sequence, 10 bases long, for a single strand of DNA (such as TACGAGTTCA).
2. Cut 10 equal-sized rectangles out of construction paper. Count how many A/T and G/C base pairs will be in your sequence. Separate the

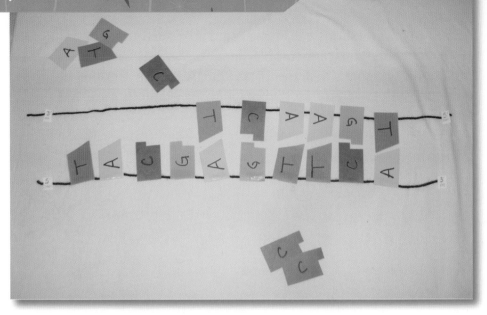

rectangles into two piles according to the number of A/T base pairs and G/C base pairs you need. Cut the A/T base-pair rectangles into two complementary shapes; cut the G/C base pair rectangles into two different complementary shapes.

3. Cut a length of yarn long enough to accommodate all your base pairs. Tape the base shapes in their sequence order along the yarn. Wrap a piece of tape around the starting end to identify it later on. Now you have one strand of DNA.

4. Play DNA polymerase. Lay your DNA strand on a table. Cut an equal length of yarn and lay it close to the bases. Match up complementary construction-paper bases, taping them to the new strand. Finally, wrap a piece of tape around the opposite end of the new strand; this is the starting end of the complementary strand. Now you have a complete, 10-base-pair double helix.

5. Repeat steps 2–4 to create two copies of the double helix. Separate your two strands and base-pairs with each of them to create two copies of your double helix sequence. Label the "top" of each strand with wrapped tape.

6. Explore the effect of a mutation. Repeat steps 2–4, but mismatch one or more of the bases. What happens to the mutation when the mismatched helix is unwound for another round of replication? What consequence might this mutation have for the cell?

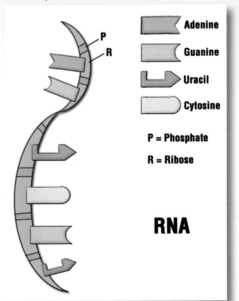

HUMAN CELL NUCLEUS

Nuclear Envelope
Outer membrane
Inner membrane
Nucleolus
Nucleoplasm
Chromatin
Heterochromatin
Euchromatin
Ribosomes
Nuclear pore

DECIPHER THE CODE OF LIFE

Like a recipe in a cookbook, a gene spells out instructions to the cell, using DNA bases in a certain order. These instructions make a specific type of protein, which performs a needed job inside an organism. But there's a catch: protein production happens outside the nucleus. How does the cell get the DNA message out?

Messenger RNA, or mRNA, solves the problem. A protein machine called RNA polymerase writes the gene-encoding stretch of DNA into a single, unpaired strand of RNA. RNA looks a lot like DNA, except that it has a ribose backbone instead of deoxyribose, and the base uracil (U) instead of thymine (T). Unlike DNA, mRNA can leave the nucleus. Once out, a group of

P
R

Adenine

Guanine

Uracil

Cytosine

P = Phosphate

R = Ribose

RNA

proteins called the **ribosome** reads the mRNA code, cooking up the called-for protein.

In 1961, a research team led by Francis Crick cracked the code. His group discovered that mRNA is broken into **codons**, or groups of three mRNA bases. Each codon codes for one of the twenty possible amino acids. Amazingly, all organisms—from bacteria to humans—use the same code.

The ribosome links the encoded amino acids together in order, like beads on a string. The long string folds up on itself to make the needed protein. See for yourself how to crack the mRNA code, and how proteins are made.

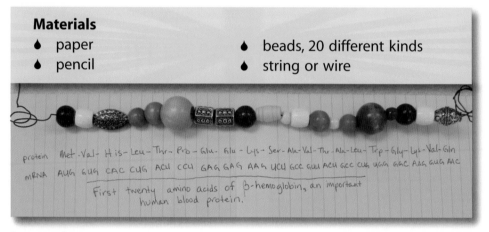

Materials
- paper
- pencil
- beads, 20 different kinds
- string or wire

protein   Met -Val- His- Leu- Thr- Pro - Glu- Glu - Lys - Ser- Ala- Val- Thr - Ala- Leu- Trp- Gly- Lys- Val- Gln
mRNA   AUG GUG CAC CUG ACU CCU GAG GAG AAG UCU GCC GUU ACU GCC CUG UGG GGC AAG GUG AAC

First twenty amino acids of β-hemoglobin, an important human blood protein.

Instructions

1. Write out an mRNA code. Start with AUG (methionine), the universal codon for "start". Continue your secret message using any combination of the four bases—A, C, G, U—in codons of three bases at a time. You can also use your 10-base DNA sequence from the previous experiment. End with any one of the three "stop" codons (UAA, UAG, or UGA).
2. Assign a different type of bead for each amino acid.
3. Translate your message from mRNA bases into "amino acid" beads.
4. String together your coded protein. It will always start with methionine. What comes next depends entirely on the code you created. Continue adding amino acid beads until you reach the end of the code.
5. Wind the string or wire to pack your amino acids together. You've just made a protein!

Second letter

First letter	U	C	A	G	Third letter
U	UUU ⎱ Phe UUC ⎰ UUA ⎱ Leu UUG ⎰	UCU ⎱ UCC ⎮ Ser UCA ⎮ UCG ⎰	UAU ⎱ Tyr UAC ⎰ UAA Stop UAG Stop	UGU ⎱ Cys UGC ⎰ UGA Stop UGG Trp	U C A G
C	CUU ⎱ CUC ⎮ Leu CUA ⎮ CUG ⎰	CCU ⎱ CCC ⎮ Pro CCA ⎮ CCG ⎰	CAU ⎱ His CAC ⎰ CAA ⎱ Gln CAG ⎰	CGU ⎱ CGC ⎮ Arg CGA ⎮ CGG ⎰	U C A G
A	AUU ⎱ AUC ⎮ Ile AUA ⎰ AUG Met	ACU ⎱ ACC ⎮ Thr ACA ⎮ ACG ⎰	AAU ⎱ Asn AAC ⎰ AAA ⎱ Lys AAG ⎰	AGU ⎱ Ser AGC ⎰ AGA ⎱ Arg AGG ⎰	U C A G
G	GUU ⎱ GUC ⎮ Val GUA ⎮ GUG ⎰	GCU ⎱ GCC ⎮ Ala GCA ⎮ GCG ⎰	GAU ⎱ Asp GAC ⎰ GAA ⎱ Glu GAG ⎰	GGU ⎱ GGC ⎮ Gly GGA ⎮ GGG ⎰	U C A G

To read the codon table, find the square where the first letter of the codon (left) meets the second letter (top). The third letter (right) points you to the correct amino acid within that square. Amino acid abbreviations are as follows: Phe=Phenylalanine; Leu=Leucine; Ile=Isoleucine; Met=Methionine; Val=Valine; Ser=Serine; Pro=Proline; Thr=Threonine; Ala=Alanine; Tyr=Tyrosine; His=Histidine; Gln=Glutamine; Asn=Asparagine; Lys=Lysine; Asp=Aspartic acid; Glu=Glutamic acid; Cys=Cysteine Trp=Tryptophan; Arg=Arginine; Gly=Glycine.

6. You might have noticed that some amino acids have more than one codon. Leucine, for example, has six. This is called **redundancy**; it helps guard against mistakes RNA polymerase or the ribosome might make. What happens when there's a mistake? Pretend RNA polymerase made a copying error and change one base in your sequence from step 1. How will it affect the protein made in step 4? Can you find places in your mRNA code where mistakes would go unnoticed? What would happen if the mistake occurred in the "start" codon? The "stop" codon?

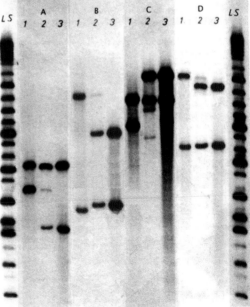

ETHICS IN GENETICS

Genetics reveals more about ourselves than we ever thought possible. With this knowledge, however, comes the ability to tamper with life in ways that have raised concern. Below are some questions that do not have easy answers. Research both sides of each situation and think carefully about what could be right, what could be wrong or dangerous, and why.

1. The FBI maintains the Combined DNA Index System (CODIS), an enormous database of genetic fingerprints. Upon entering prison, every U.S. inmate must submit a DNA sample to CODIS. Unsolved cases with DNA evidence are screened against the inmates' DNA. In 2008 alone, DNA sequences stored on CODIS helped solve 66,783 investigations. But critics

Genetic fingerprint

40

DNA Profiling

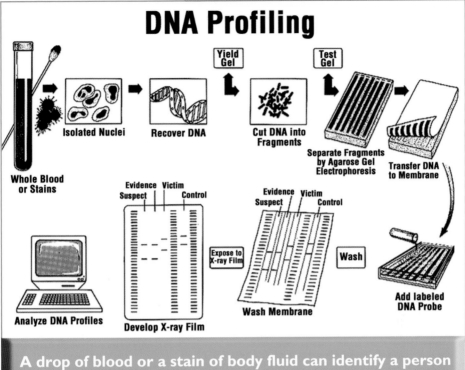

Yield Gel

Test Gel

Isolated Nuclei

Recover DNA

Cut DNA into Fragments

Separate Fragments by Agarose Gel Electrophoresis

Transfer DNA to Membrane

Whole Blood or Stains

Evidence Victim
Suspect | | Control

Evidence Victim
Suspect / / Control

Expose to X-ray Film

Wash

Add labeled DNA Probe

Analyze DNA Profiles

Develop X-ray Film

Wash Membrane

A drop of blood or a stain of body fluid can identify a person by his or her DNA. Forensic scientists isolate the DNA (much like you did on page 22), make copies using DNA polymerase in a test tube, and run tests to determine its sequence. Like fingerprints, no two DNA samples are alike.

believe that the FBI violates the prisoners' right to privacy by forcing them to give their genetic fingerprint, which will stay in CODIS forever. What do you think?

2. Genetically modified (GM) plants contain foreign pieces of DNA. Monsanto corn has a gene that helps it survive an onslaught of pesticide. The Flavr Savr tomato has a coldwater-fish gene that helps it stay ripe on store shelves. Golden rice, engineered to produce vitamin A, is given to farmers in impoverished countries to combat poor nutrition.

Some geneticists argue that GM plants use less land and less energy to help feed a starving world. GM opponents, however, worry that the engineered genes can transfer to other plants, with unknown results. Ecologists also point out that world hunger may be a result of bad governments, not bad farming. What do you think?

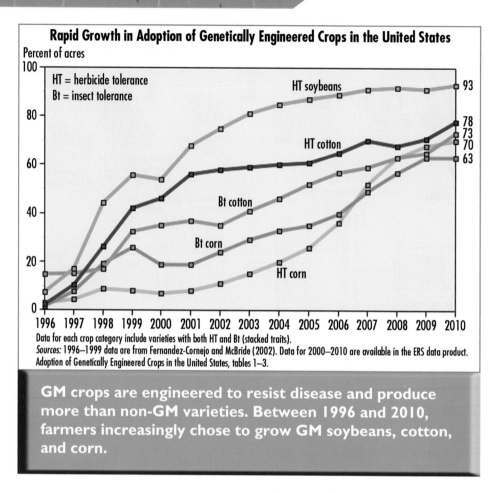

Rapid Growth in Adoption of Genetically Engineered Crops in the United States

Percent of acres

HT = herbicide tolerance
Bt = insect tolerance

HT soybeans — 93

HT cotton — 78 / 73 / 70 / 63

Bt cotton

Bt corn

HT corn

Data for each crop category include varieties with both HT and Bt (stacked traits).
Sources: 1996–1999 data are from Fernandez-Cornejo and McBride (2002). Data for 2000–2010 are available in the ERS data product. Adoption of Genetically Engineered Crops in the United States, tables 1–3.

GM crops are engineered to resist disease and produce more than non-GM varieties. Between 1996 and 2010, farmers increasingly chose to grow GM soybeans, cotton, and corn.

3. Dolly the Sheep, the first cloned mammal, was cloned in 1996 and born in 1997. Cloning is still a new technology with very low success rates, but creating new life in a lab is highly controversial. Can you identify the pros and cons of each side? Which do you agree with and why?

   a. Proponents argue that human cloning, through stem-cell research, can create organs for patients who need them. Wildlife biologists hope that cloning may give a future to endangered or extinct animals.

   b. Cloning opponents worry that the technology could easily go too far, abusing life while creating it. Movies popularize this concern, from the dinosaurs in *Jurassic Park* to clone troopers in *Star Wars*. Should cloning get too advanced, opponents worry that human parents will want designer

Dolly the Sheep, who lived until 2003, was cloned at the Roslin Institute in Scotland from a female domestic sheep's mammary gland cell. The same cloning techniques have since been used by researchers all over the world to clone cattle, deer, goats, pigs, cats, rabbits, and mice.

babies, creating a world that prizes certain genetic traits over others.

4. Some potential parents are at high risk of having a baby with birth defects or fatal genetic diseases. They choose to have pre-natal (pre-birth) genetic screening. Samples of their DNA are analyzed before or during pregnancy to determine the proba-bility of their child's inheriting a deadly disease.

   a. Research some of these genetic diseases, such as Tay-Sachs disease, cystic fibrosis, and sickle-cell anemia. What are the pros and cons of prenatal genetic screening?

   b. Some insurance companies require prenatal screening, and they may refuse to cover medical costs for an anticipated special-needs child. Consider the issue from both the par-ents' side and the insurance company's side.

Books

Harvey, Derek, Kim Bryan, and Trevor Day. *Biology Matters! Genetics.* Danbury, CT: Grolier, 2004.

Hunter, William. *DNA Analysis.* Philadelphia: Mason Crest Publishers, 2005.

McLeish, Ewan. *Genetic Revolution.* Mankato, MN: Stargazer Books, 2007.

Silverstein, Alvin, Virginia Silverstein, and Laura Silverstein Nunn. *DNA.* Minneapolis, MN: Twenty-First Century Books, 2008.

Works Consulted

Campbell, Neil A. *Biology.* Menlo Park, CA: The Benjamin/Cummings Publication Company, Inc., 1996.

Dahm, Ralf. "The First Discovery of DNA". *American Scientist*, July-August 2008, p. 320. http://www.americanscientist.org/issues/page2/the-first-discovery-of-dna

DNA and the Criminal Justice System. Ed. David Lazer. Cambridge, MA: The M.I.T. Press, 2004.

Genetics and Heredity. Ed. John Clark. New York: Torstar Books, 1985.

"Genetics Experiments to Do at Home." http://www.blisstree.com/geneticsandhealth/genetics-experiments-to-do-at-home/

"Make a Model DNA Strand." http://dnamazing.com/media/how-to-make-a-dna-model.pdf

Mendel, Gregor. "Experiments in Plant Hybridization." 1865. http://www.mendelweb.org/Mendel.html

Nexus Research Group. "DNA and Genetic Engineering." http://www.nexusresearchgroup.com/fun_science/dna.htm.

Ridley, Matt. *Genome.* New York: HarperCollins, 1999.

Snustad, Peter, Michael J. Simmons, John B. Jenkins. *Principles of Genetics.* New York: John Wiley & Sons, Inc., 1997.

University of Georgia Savannah River Ecology Laboratory. "Kids Do Science: Probability and Genetics." http://www.uga.edu/srel/kidsdoscience/kidsdoscience-genetics.htm

Watson, James D. *DNA: The Secret of Life.* New York: Alfred A. Knopf, 2003.

————. *The Double Helix.* New York: Touchstone, 2001.

Willett, Edward. *Genetics Demystified.* New York: McGraw-Hill, 2005.

Windelspecht, Michael. *Genetics 101.* Westport, CT: Greenwood Press, 2007.

On the Internet

DNA from the Beginning
    http://www.dnaftb.org/dnaftb/1/concept/index.html
The GEEE! In Genome
    http://nature.ca/genome/04/041/041_e.cfm
The Genetics Education Center
    http://www.kumc.edu/gec/
Learn. Genetics.
    http://learn.genetics.utah.edu/
"Pea Soup" Pea Experiment
    http://sonic.net/~nbs/projects/anthro201/exper/
A Science Odyssey: You Try It: DNA Workshop
    http://www.pbs.org/wgbh/aso/tryit/dna/#

GLOSSARY

allele (uh-LEEL)—One variety of a specific gene.

anaphase (AN-uh-fayz)—Third stage in mitosis. The two chromosome copies are pulled apart to opposite sides of the cell.

base—In DNA, one of four varieties of stable molecules (Adenine, Thymine, Guanine, Cytosine) that make up the "rungs."

centromere (SEN-troh-meer)—A protein structure that temporarily joins two copies of a chromosome during mitosis.

chromosome (KROH-moh-zohm)—A continuous stretch of DNA. Human body cells have 46 chromosomes.

clone (KLOHN)—A genetic copy.

codon (KOH-don)—Three consecutive bases of mRNA that code for a specific amino acid, or for the end of a protein.

cross—To fertilize one plant with pollen from another.

deoxyribonucleic acid (dee-OK-see-ry-boh-noo-KLAY-ik AA-sid)—A chemical found in every cell and some viruses that passes genetic information from one generation to the next. Also known as DNA.

DNA polymerase (pah-LIM-uh-rays)—A group of proteins responsible for copying DNA.

dominant (DAH-mih-nunt)—In genetics, an allele that can mask a recessive trait.

gamete (GAM-eet)—A reproductive cell that contains half the DNA needed to make a new organism.

genes (JEENS)—Sections of DNA that code for proteins.

geneticist (jeh-NEH-tih-sist)—A biologist who specializes in studying genetics.

genome (JEE-nohm)—The complete set of DNA instructions found within an organism.

genotype (JEE-noh-typ)—Genes in an allele that work together to create a phenotype.

heterozygous (heh-tuh-roh-ZY-gus)—Containing two different alleles for a specific gene.

homozygous (HOH-moh-zy-gus)—Containing two identical alleles for a specific gene.

hybrid (HY-brid)—A cross between two different types.

meiosis (my-OH-sis)—Cell division that creates gametes containing exactly half of the genetic material required to make a body cell.

metaphase (MEH-teh-fayz)—Second stage in mitosis. All chromosomes line up in the center of the cell.

mitosis (my-TOH-sis)—Process by which a cell reproduces itself, passing along a full and correct copy of its DNA.

molecular (moh-LEK-yoo-lur)—On the size or nature of molecules.

mutations (myoo-TAY-shuns)—Changes in DNA.

nucleus (NOO-klee-us)—Part of a cell that stores DNA.

phenotype (FEE-noh-typ)—Physical trait created by a combination of alleles (for example, blue eyes, freckles, blood type).

prophase (PROH-fayz)—First stage in mitosis. Chromosomes pack tightly. Chromosome copies join loosely. The nuclear wall breaks down.

recessive (ree-SEH-siv)—In genetics, an allele whose presence is usually masked by a dominant variety.

redundancy (ree-DUN-dun-see)—Repetitiveness to guard against mistakes.

ribosome (RY-boh-zohm)—A group of proteins that reads mRNA (messenger ribonucleic acid) to make proteins.

sister chromatids (KROH-muh-tids)—Chromosome copies.

telophase (TEH-luh-fayz)—Fourth and final stage in mitosis. The cell divides. New nuclear walls form around each set of chromosomes.

traits (TRAYTS)—Inherited characteristics.

Claire O'Neal holds degrees in English and biology from Indiana University, and a Ph.D. in chemistry from the University of Washington. In addition to professional scientific papers, she has written over a dozen books for Mitchell Lane Publishers, including *Exploring Earth's Biomes* in this series and *Volcanoes*, *Earthquakes*, and *Rocks and Minerals* in the series Earth Science Projects for Kids. When she isn't spending time with her husband and two young sons, she enjoys concocting mad science experiments in her kitchen.